YOUNG REPORTER IN FRANCE

SPECIAL DAYS AND HOLIDAYS

Jours de fête

SUE FINNIE AND DANIÈLE BOURDAIS

W

FRANKLIN WATTS

LONDON • SYDNEY

This edition 2014

Franklin Watts
338 Euston Road
London NW1 3BH

Franklin Watts Australia
Level 17/207 Kent Street
Sydney, NSW 2000

Series editor: Sarah Peutrill
Art Director: Jonathan Hair
Designer: Graham Rich
Photo manager: Véronique Bussolin
Photographs by Paul Villecourt, unless otherwise specified
Text consultant: Fabrice Blanchefort

Thanks to Carine Bourgogne and Fabrice Blanchefort for
their contribution to the audio recordings

Credits: Andrey Armyagov/Shutterstock: 3cl, 5t, 23tr. Ingrid Balabanova/Shutterstock:
12cr. G Beauland/Shutterstock: 3tr, 24c. Beata Becla/Shutterstock: 12br. Andrew
Buckin/Shutterstock: 11cr. Cuboimages/Alamy: 14bl. Derek Gordon/Shutterstock: 24t.
hfng/Shutterstock: 20bl. iwka/Shutterstock: 4cr, 22c. Kaktuzoiv/Shutterstock: 11t. Jules
Kitano/Shutterstock: 16br. Kurhan/Shutterstock: 11br. Phillip Lange/Shutterstock: 23c.
Christina McWilliams/Shutterstock: 4b, 20br, 28bl. Madeleine Openshaw/Shutterstock:
16cl, 29t. Kirsty Pargeter/Shutterstock: 15t. Alistair Scott/Shutterstock: 15b, 28cr.
Sharpner/Shutterstock: 22br. Maria Sidelnikova & Vitaly Titov/Shutterstock: 3tl, 13tr.
Southwind/Shutterstock: 1, 18cl. Sandra van der Steen/Shutterstock: 18t. K Thorson/
Shutterstock: 21tr. Timmary/Shutterstock: 22bl. Vnlit/Shutterstock: 13tc. Hsinli Wang/
istockphoto: 25. Lisa F. Young/Shutterstock: 2tr, 4tr, 5cl, 9tr, 14tl. Zurijeta/Shutterstock:
18cr. Every attempt has been made to clear copyright.
Should there be any inadvertent omission please apply
to the publisher for rectification.

Dewey number: 394.2'6944
ISBN: 978 1 4451 3215 0
Printed in China

Franklin Watts is a division of Hachette Children's Books,
an Hachette UK company.
www.hachette.co.uk

Please note:
The names of the children featured in this book
have been changed.

The children's answers to the young reporter's
questions are personal and it should not be
assumed that all children in France experience
special days and holidays in exactly the same way.

CONTENTS

Sections marked with this symbol have free audio clips available at www.franklinwatts.co.uk/downloads

Ryan

MEET RYAN, OUR YOUNG REPORTER IN FRANCE

Meet Ryan. He is in France on a special mission. He is going to find out all about special days and holidays in France. He has lots of questions.

What do children do on their birthdays?

Do they have Hallowe'en in France?

Do they eat Easter bunnies at Easter?

Which day do children watch fireworks?

What do French children do during the summer holidays?

Is it true they eat their Christmas dinner at midnight?

Read on and find out the answers to these questions... *and lots more!*

BIENVENUE EN FRANCE!

Welcome to France. The little town of Crest is in south-east France. Meet some children who live there.

Antoine is 11.

He lives with his mum and dad and his two sisters.

He likes making pancakes… and eating them!

In summer, he goes canoeing with his friends.

Antoine

Romain

Romain is 12.

He lives with his parents and younger brother, Léo.

He speaks two languages: French and English.

Every summer, he goes to summer camp.

Léo is 9.

He lives with his mum, dad and big brother, Romain.

His favourite day of the year is Christmas Day.

Like his brother, he can speak French and English.

Léo

Did you know?

There are 11 official bank holidays in France every year.

Carine is 10.

She and her sister live with their grandparents.

Her favourite outing is going to the park with her friends.

She likes shopping too... especially for sweets!

Carine

You can practise your French and learn some new words as you find out what these children have to say. All the French words are translated on pages 30–31.

MON JOUR PRÉFÉRÉ

It's Romain's birthday. He is 12 today. Our young reporter is interviewing him to find out all about his special day.

Young reporter: **Bon anniversaire, Romain! Qu'est-ce que tu as eu pour ton anniversaire?**

Romain: **Pour mon anniversaire, j'ai eu des cartes, des cadeaux et de l'argent. C'est génial!**

Pour mon anniversaire, j'ai eu un jeu vidéo.

Romain's birthday is on 25 June (**le vingt-cinq juin**). It's definitely his favourite day of the year. He invites a few friends round for a special birthday tea, with a cake and candles. This year, he has quite a few cards and presents and some money (**30 euros**) from his grandparents.

J'ai eu un gâteau, avec des bougies.

USEFUL PHRASES

Bon anniversaire! Happy birthday! **Qu'est-ce que tu as eu?** What did you get?
pour ton anniversaire for your birthday **des cartes** some cards
des cadeaux some presents **de l'argent** some money **C'est génial!** It's great!
un gâteau a cake **avec des bougies** with candles **un jeu vidéo** a computer game

Romain and his friend wear scary costumes at Hallowe'en!

As well as their birthday, French children have another special day every year: their name day (**la fête**). In France, every day of the year is named after a different saint. When it is the celebration of the saint with the same name as you, it is your 'name day'. Romain's name day is on 28 February (**le vingt-huit février**) – the celebration of Saint Romain. Just like a mini-birthday, on that day he might get more cards and money (and sometimes presents too)!

Romain loves Hallowe'en (**Halloween**) too, even though this is not a traditional French celebration. Over the past 20 years, more and more French people have been following the American customs of Hallowe'en. Shops decorate their displays with carved pumpkins (**des citrouilles**), witches (**des sorcières**) and

French children make decorations for Hallowe'en.

bats (**des chauves-souris**). Children enjoy dressing up in scary costumes: on the evening of 31 October, you might well see ghosts (**des fantômes**), witches or vampires (**des vampires**) wandering the streets of any French town!

What did you have for your birthday?

cards (**des cartes**)   presents (**des cadeaux**)   money (**de l'argent**)
a cake (**un gâteau**)   candles (**des bougies**)   balloons (**des ballons**)
a party (**une boum**)   a special meal (**un repas spécial**)

YOUR TURN

Et toi? Qu'est-ce que tu as eu pour ton anniversaire? Complète.

Pour mon anniversaire, j'ai eu...

The French birthday song is sung to the same tune as 'Happy Birthday to you':

Joyeux anniversaire,
Joyeux anniversaire

Joyeux anniversaire*,
Joyeux anniversaire

(*sometimes the person's name is squeezed in here).

THE FRENCH CALENDAR

Here are some important dates in the French year.

Le Jour de l'An (New Year's Day) is the first day of the new year. Time to make a New Year's resolution!

La Chandeleur (Candlemas) is the day when French people make pancakes and toss them for good luck!

La Fête Nationale (Bastille Day). 14 July is France's national day, with fireworks and celebrations.

janvier						
Lu	Ma	Me	Je	Ve	Sa	Di
					1	2
3	4	5	6	7	8	9
10	11	12	13	14	15	16
17	18	19	20	21	22	23
24	25	26	27	28	29	30
31						

février						
Lu	Ma	Me	Je	Ve	Sa	Di
	1	2	3	4	5	6
7	8	9	10	11	12	13
14	15	16	17	18	19	20
21	22	23	24	25	26	27
28						

avril						
Lu	Ma	Me	Je	Ve	Sa	Di
				1	2	3
4	5	6	7	8	9	10
11	12	13	14	15	16	17
18	19	20	21	22	23	24
25	26	27	28	29	30	

mai						
Lu	Ma	Me	Je	Ve	Sa	Di
						1
2	3	4	5	6	7	8
9	10	11	12	13	14	15
16	17	18	19	20	21	22
23	24	25	26	27	28	29
30	31					

juillet						
Lu	Ma	Me	Je	Ve	Sa	Di
				1	2	3
4	5	6	7	8	9	10
11	12	13	14	15	16	17
18	19	20	21	22	23	24
25	26	27	28	29	30	31

août						
Lu	Ma	Me	Je	Ve	Sa	Di
1	2	3	4	5	6	7
8	9	10	11	12	13	14
15	16	17	18	19	20	21
22	23	24	25	26	27	28
29	30	31				

octobre						
Lu	Ma	Me	Je	Ve	Sa	Di
					1	2
3	4	5	6	7	8	9
10	11	12	13	14	15	16
17	18	19	20	21	22	23
24	25	26	27	28	29	30
31						

novembre						
Lu	Ma	Me	Je	Ve	Sa	Di
	1	2	3	4	5	6
7	8	9	10	11	12	13
14	15	16	17	18	19	20
21	22	23	24	25	26	27
28	29	30				

Did you know?

French organisations like the post office (**la Poste**) and the fire brigade (**les sapeurs-pompiers**) often produce and sell calendars to the public to raise money.

La Toussaint (All Saints' Day), the day after Hallowe'en, is a public holiday in France.

mars						
Lu	Ma	Me	Je	Ve	Sa	Di
	1	2	3	4	5	6
7	8	9	10	11	12	13
14	15	16	17	18	19	20
21	22	23	24	25	26	27
28	29	30	31			

Pâques (Easter) falls on a different date each year, usually in March or April. French children eat Easter eggs or chocolate animals.

juin						
Lu	Ma	Me	Je	Ve	Sa	Di
		1	2	3	4	5
6	7	8	9	10	11	12
13	14	15	16	17	18	19
20	21	22	23	24	25	26
27	28	29	30			

Le feu de la Saint-Jean (Midsummer's Day). The French celebrate the middle of summer by building huge bonfires.

septembre						
Lu	Ma	Me	Je	Ve	Sa	Di
			1	2	3	4
5	6	7	8	9	10	11
12	13	14	15	16	17	18
19	20	21	22	23	24	25
26	27	28	29	30		

La rentrée (back-to-school) is the day in early September when French children go back to school after the summer holidays.

décembre						
Lu	Ma	Me	Je	Ve	Sa	Di
			1	2	3	4
5	6	7	8	9	10	11
12	13	14	15	16	17	18
19	20	21	22	23	24	25
26	27	28	29	30	31	

Noël (Christmas) is a time for family reunions and presents. Christians sometimes go to Midnight Mass at church.

MINI-QUIZ

Can you match the days to the greetings?

1 birthday

2 name day

3 Christmas

4 Easter

5 New Year's Day

a Bonne fête!

b Joyeux Noël!

c Bonne année!

d Joyeux anniversaire!

e Joyeuses Pâques!

MINI-QUIZ ANSWERS

1d, 2a, 3b, 4e, 5c

EXTRA CHALLENGE

Make your own French calendar. Don't forget to include birthdays – your own and your friends'!

C'EST NOËL!

Léo's favourite day is Christmas. Today he is telling our young reporter Ryan why it is so much fun.

Young reporter: **Qu'est-ce que tu fais à Noël, Léo?**

Léo: **On décore un grand sapin de Noël. C'est beau!**

Et on a des cadeaux de Noël!

The celebration of Christmas in France varies from family to family and from region to region. Most people celebrate Christmas on 25 December, which is a public holiday (**un jour férié**). There is no French equivalent of Boxing Day: most people go back to work on 26 December.

On décore la maison.

J'ai des cadeaux de Noël. J'adore les cadeaux!

USEFUL PHRASES

Qu'est-ce que tu fais... What do you do... **à Noël** at Christmas
on décore we decorate **un sapin de Noël** a Christmas tree **c'est beau!** it's beautiful!
on a we have **des cadeaux de Noël** Christmas presents
la maison the house **j'ai** I have **j'adore** I love

MY BLOG
What is Christmas like at Léo's house?

Léo loves helping to put up decorations for Christmas. The Christmas tree (**le sapin de Noël**) is his favourite. There are hardly any Christmas cards to put up because most French people send their greetings at New Year instead.

Léo's mum makes a special Christmas lunch: there are oysters (**des huîtres**) to start, then a big turkey (**la dinde**) or goose (**l'oie**). But for Léo, the best is dessert: chocolate log (**la bûche de Noël**).

The Christmas excitement is all too much for Léo's dog, Taz.

On Christmas Eve (**la veille de Noël**), Léo leaves out a shoe by the fireside. He always wakes up really early on Christmas morning to see if Father Christmas (**le Père Noël**) has filled his shoe with sweets and little presents. He gets presents from his mum and dad, his grandparents and his aunt and uncle too. They are left under the tree and opened before breakfast.

What do you do at Christmas?

we put up decorations (**on décore la maison**)
we have a Christmas tree (**on a un sapin de Noël**)
we have Christmas presents (**on a des cadeaux de Noël**)
we have a special meal (**on a un repas spécial**)

YOUR TURN

Et toi? Qu'est-ce que tu fais à Noël?

À Noël, chez moi, on...

In French, 'on' can mean different things. It can mean 'we' or 'people in general'.

CHRISTMAS AND NEW YEAR IN FRANCE

In France, Christmas starts early.

In parts of north and east France, **le Père Noël** comes early, on 6 December, the feast day of **Saint Nicolas**, bringing presents and sweets.

In the city of Lyon, celebrations start on 8 December. This is marked by the Festival of Lights (**la fête des lumières**), when people put candles in their windows to light up the city.

Nativity scenes (**des crèches**) showing the birth of the baby Jesus (**l'enfant Jésus**) are popular Christmas decorations in homes, shops and often as street displays.

In Provence in the south of France, nativity scenes are usually made with little painted pottery figures, known as '**santons**', little saints (right).

Did you know?

French people used to have their Christmas dinner, called **le réveillon**, when they got back from Midnight Mass on Christmas Eve. Some people still eat their special Christmas dinner on Christmas Eve instead of Christmas Day.

New Year's Eve (31 December) is called **la Saint-Sylvestre** in France. There is usually a big feast (**le Réveillon de la Saint-Sylvestre**) and sometimes a party where everyone stays up until after midnight to welcome the new year.

On New Year's Day, people make their New Year's resolutions. Adults give children a little extra pocket money (**des étrennes**). During January people often send little cards with good wishes for the coming year.

Did you know?

In France, at midnight on New Year's Eve, people kiss under the mistletoe for good luck and wish each other a Happy New Year (**Bonne année!**).

MINI-QUIZ

These things are all linked to New Year in France. Can you guess what they are?

1 une bonne résolution
- a happy new year?
- a New Year's resolution?
- a good meal?

2 le Jour de l'An
- Christmas Eve?
- New Year's Eve?
- New Year's Day?

3 le gui
- mistletoe?
- holly?
- streamers?

MINI-QUIZ ANSWERS

3 mistletoe

2 New Year's Day

1 a New Year's resolution

EXTRA CHALLENGE

The French version of Jingle Bells is sung to the same tune. Can you sing it?

Vive le vent, vive le vent,
vive le vent d'hiver
Qui s'en va sifflant, soufflant
Dans les grands sapins verts...
Oh ! Vive le temps, vive le temps,
vive le temps d'hiver
Boule de neige et jour
de l'an Et bonne année
grand-mère...

LES FÊTES D'HIVER

Today our young reporter is interviewing Antoine to find out about some special winter celebrations.

Young reporter: **Antoine, chez toi, il y a des fêtes en hiver?**

Antoine: **Oui. En hiver, il y a la Fête des Rois. Cette année, j'ai eu la fève.**

La galette des rois, c'est bon!

The Festival of the Three Kings (**la Fête des Rois** or **Épiphanie**) is on 6 January. According to Christian tradition, this is the day the three kings came to visit the baby Jesus.

People eat a large cake or pie called kings' cake (**la galette des rois**). Hidden in the cake is a charm (**la fève**). If you find the charm in your piece of cake, you are the King or Queen for the day, and wear a paper crown.

La couronne

USEFUL PHRASES

chez toi where you live   **il y a des fêtes?** are there any celebrations?
en hiver in winter   **oui** yes   **il y a** there's   **la Fête des Rois** festival of the three kings
Épiphanie Epiphany   **cette année** this year   **j'ai eu** I got   **la fève** the charm
la couronne the crown   **c'est bon!** it's good!

The Christian holiday of Candlemas (**la Chandeleur**) is on 2 February. Antoine told me that in France this is the day French people traditionally eat pancakes (**les crêpes**).

Antoine helps his mum to make the pancakes. They always have a good laugh tossing the pancakes to turn them over. You have to be very careful not to drop them! According to tradition, if you can flip the pancake and catch it while holding a gold coin in your hand, you will have good luck for the rest of the year.

Tossing pancakes is not that easy!

Antoine said he has fun making the pancakes, but what he really looks forward to is eating them!

French people make pancakes on Shrove Tuesday (**le Mardi gras**) too.

More autumn and winter celebrations

Eid-ul-Fitr (**l'Aïd el-Fitr**)   Yom Kippur (**Yom Kippour**)   Diwali (**Divali**)
Remembrance Day (**l'Armistice**)   Hanukkah (**la fête du Chanukah**)
Chinese New Year (**le Nouvel An chinois**)   Valentine's Day (**la Saint-Valentin**)
Carnival (**le carnaval**)

YOUR TURN

Chez toi, il y a des fêtes en hiver?

Chez moi, il y a...

There are little symbols called 'accents' above some letters in French.

Did you spot the one that looks like an upside-down v in **fête** and **crêpe**? This is called a circumflex.

AUTUMN AND WINTER CELEBRATIONS

All Saints' Day (**la Toussaint**) is a Christian holiday on 1 November. It is the tradition for families to visit the cemetery to pay their respects to relatives who have died. They put chrysanthemums on their graves. In France, these flowers are associated with death, so people never give them as a gift.

Did you know?

In France, there is no Bonfire Night or fireworks on 5 November.

Mardi gras (**le Mardi gras**) literally means 'fat Tuesday'. It is also carnival time (**le carnaval**) in France. There are parades in the street with colourful floats and people in fancy dress. The largest celebration is in the city of Nice, where the celebrations last for 12 days.

Eid-ul-Fitr (**l'Aïd el-Fitr**) is a Muslim festival marking the end of the fast of Ramadan. After Christianity, Islam is the second most widely practised religion in France, so Eid is an important celebration there. Antoine's friend Nejma loves to celebrate Eid with her family and Muslim neighbours.

Valentine's Day (**la Saint-Valentin**) is on 14 February. People send cards decorated with hearts to say 'I love you' (**Je t'aime**). If you get a card with no name, it means you have a secret admirer!

Did you know?

The European Day of Languages (**la Journée européenne des langues**) is on 26 September.

MINI-QUIZ

Can you guess the correct answers?

1 Mardi Gras takes place 46 days before which festival?
- Christmas
- Valentine's Day
- Easter

2 Which American city is famous for its **Mardi Gras** festival?
- New Orleans
- New York
- Washington

3 What happens at **la bataille des fleurs** at the Nice carnival?
- people grow flowers
- people throw flowers at each other
- people pick flowers

MINI-QUIZ ANSWERS

3 people throw flowers

2 New Orleans

1 Easter

EXTRA CHALLENGE

Can you find the city of Nice on a map of France?

(clue: It's in the south.)

LA FÊTE NATIONALE

Today Ryan is interviewing Carine about France's national holiday: Bastille Day.

Young reporter: **Salut, Carine! Ton pays a une fête nationale?**

Carine: **Oui! En France, la Fête Nationale, c'est le quatorze juillet.**

Il y a des défilés, des bals, des feux d'artifice... et des pétards!

On Bastille Day, French people remember the storming of the Bastille prison in Paris at the start of the French Revolution, back in 1789. By capturing the prison, the ordinary people showed how angry they were at the way the King was treating them.

They coined the slogan **Liberté, égalité, fraternité!** (Freedom, equality, brotherhood!).

Le drapeau tricolore est un symbole de la Révolution française.

Le quatorze juillet, il y a des feux d'artifice en France.

USEFUL PHRASES

ton pays your country   **une fête nationale** a national holiday
c'est le quatorze juillet it's on 14 July   **il y a** there are   **des défilés** parades
des bals dances   **des feux d'artifice** firework displays   **des pétards** bangers (fireworks)
le drapeau tricolore the French flag   **la Révolution française** the French Revolution

Carine says there are lots of good things about 14 July. All over France there are parades with brass bands (**des fanfares**) and people marching. The biggest parade of all is the military one in Paris. It's in the long, wide avenue called the **Champs-Elysées**. Carine has never been to Paris, but she likes to watch the parade on TV. The horses (**les chevaux**) are her favourite thing.

In the evening of 14 July (and the evening before), there are dances in the street and firework displays in big cities, small towns and villages.

It sounds fun, but Carine says to watch out for firecrackers (**les pétards**). Children are allowed to buy them, and they let them off all day long. They make a terrible loud bang, which can really make you jump!

What can you see on Bastille Day?

fireworks (**les feux d'artifice**)   dances in the street (**les bals du 14 juillet**)
the French flag (**le drapeau tricolore**)   brass bands (**les fanfares**)
parades (**les défilés**)

YOUR TURN

Ton pays a une fête nationale?

✓ *Oui, c'est le...* (+ date)

✗ *Non.*

In French, there are three different words for 'the': **le, la and les. Les** is always used in front of a plural word.

SPRING AND SUMMER CELEBRATIONS

April Fool's Day (Poisson d'avril)

The first of April is a day for practical jokes in France. The traditional trick is to cut out a paper fish. You have to try to stick it to your victim's back without them noticing. Then you run away fast, calling out **Poisson d'avril!** (April fish!).

Easter (Pâques)

On Easter Sunday, French children get Easter eggs (**les œufs de Pâques**). Some families hide the eggs in the garden or around the house and the children have to hunt for them. There are chocolate rabbits, chicks and bells too. Easter Monday is a public holiday, so most people have the day off.

1 May (Le premier mai)

It's the tradition to give your friends or family a little bunch of lily of the valley (**le muguet**) on this day to bring them good luck.

Music Day (la fête de la musique)

On 21 June, there are free concerts with all kinds of music.

Mother's Day (la fête des mères)

Mother's Day is the last Sunday of May in France. This is a private, rather than a public, celebration. Children give their mum a card or a present as a thank-you for all the things she does for them. The greeting on the card is: **Bonne fête, Maman!** Sometimes they have lunch at a restaurant so that Mum doesn't have to do the cooking or washing-up!

*Antoine and his sisters always give their mum a card for **la fête des mères**.*

Did you know?

In France, Father's Day (**la fête des pères**) comes two or three weeks after **la fête des mères**.

MINI-QUIZ

Can you guess what French people eat at Easter time?

1 On Good Friday
- fish (**du poisson**)?
- chicken (**du poulet**)?
- sausages (**des saucisses**)?

2 On Easter Sunday
- lamb (**de l'agneau**)?
- beef (**du bœuf**)?
- duck (**du canard**)?

3 How many Easter eggs does the average French 11-year -old eat?
- 3
- 7
- 13

MINI-QUIZ ANSWERS

3 13

2 lamb (de l'agneau)

1 fish (du poisson)

EXTRA CHALLENGE

Make a French greetings card for Easter (**Joyeuses Pâques!**) or for Mother's Day (**Bonne fête, Maman!**) or Father's Day (**Bonne fête, Papa!**).

LES VACANCES D'ÉTÉ

Today our young reporter is interviewing Romain about the summer holidays.

Young reporter: **Romain, quelle est ton activité préférée pendant les grandes vacances?**

Romain: **Pendant les grandes vacances, j'aime me reposer. En juillet, je vais en colonie de vacances. C'est génial!**

J'aime faire du bricolage avec mon père.

French children are lucky enough to have two months' holiday from school in the summer (July and August). Some children go away with their family or to a summer camp. But one in three stay at home. In the town of Crest where Romain lives, the weather is usually hot and sunny in the summer, so he likes to go swimming or relax in the garden.

Je fais du canoë avec mes amis.

USEFUL PHRASES

quelle est... ? what is...?   **ton activité préférée** your favourite activity   **pendant** during
les grandes vacances the summer holidays   **j'aime me reposer** I like to relax   **en juillet** in July
je vais en colonie de vacances I go to summer camp   **c'est génial** it's great
faire du bricolage doing odd jobs (DIY)   **avec mon père** with my dad
je fais du canoë I go canoeing   **avec mes amis** with my friends

Every year in July, Romain and his brother go to summer camp (**une colonie de vacances**). Their parents stay at home and the children are looked after for two or three weeks by playleaders (**les moniteurs**) who organise outings and activities. Romain enjoys being away from home and trying lots of different activities. This year he had a go at snorkelling (**la plongée avec un tuba**).

Learning to snorkel.

In August, Romain went on holiday with his mum and dad and his brother. They went to a campsite in the Camargue region in the south of France.

It was the ideal holiday for Romain: he loves camping and he loves the Camargue, where you can see flamingos (**des flamands roses**) and white horses (**des chevaux blancs**) roaming wild.

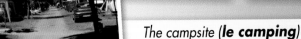

*The campsite (**le camping**)*

Popular summer activities

football (**le football**) swimming (**la natation**) tennis (**le tennis**)
skateboarding (**le skateboard**) going to the beach (**aller à la plage**)
playing with friends (**jouer avec les amis**) shopping (**faire du shopping**)
having a day out (**faire une excursion**)

YOUR TURN

Et toi? Quelle est ton activité préférée pendant les grandes vacances?

• J'aime...

Some of the French names for activities look the same (or almost) as English. But they don't sound the same! Listen to the audio to find out the correct way to say them.

THE SUMMER HOLIDAYS

The French love to be beside the seaside!

French people usually stay in France for their holidays. Only one in three holiday-makers goes abroad (mainly to Spain or North Africa).

Enjoying the beach in Cannes, southern France.

Where do French holiday-makers go?

The Roman amphitheatre in Arles, Provence is a popular tourist spot.

56%	seaside	(**au bord de la mer**)
17%	countryside	(**à la campagne**)
12%	mountains	(**à la montagne**)
11%	town/city	(**en ville**)
4%	lake	(**au bord d'un lac**)

0   20   40   60   80   100%

Did you know?

French holiday-makers love a holiday by the sea, but more than a quarter of them can't swim.

France is a great place for holidays. It has beaches in the north, the south and the west, mountains in the south-west and the east, and lots of countryside and interesting towns, like Arles with its Roman amphitheatre (above).

Paris plage

Paris – the capital of France – is not by the sea. But for one month every summer the seaside comes to the city! Sand and palm trees are brought in to make a tropical beach along the banks of the River Seine in Paris. It's called Paris beach (**Paris plage**) and it's almost as good as the real thing! There are deckchairs, ice-cream sellers and beach volleyball. At the **Bassin de la Villette**, there are pedaloes and rowing boats too.

Paris plage

Did you know?

People haven't always had summer holidays. Paid time off work was not a right for workers in France until 1936.

MINI-QUIZ

Can you guess the correct answers?

1 Which town is by the sea?

- Paris
- Cannes
- Crest

2 Where would you go for a mountain holiday?

- the Alps
- the Camargue
- Brittany

3 What is the name of the train that takes tourists from London to Paris?

- TGV
- Eurostar
- Eurotunnel

MINI-QUIZ ANSWERS

3 Eurostar

2 the Alps

1 Cannes

EXTRA CHALLENGE

Can you name any other French holiday destinations?

TEST YOUR MEMORY!

1 When do you say Bon anniversaire?
- on New Year's Day
- on someone's birthday
- on Mother's Day

2 What do French children eat for la Chandeleur?
- sweets
- chocolate eggs
- pancakes

3 Which day is Bastille Day?

- 14 February
- 14 July
- 26 December

4 Who is le Père Noël?
- a carnival character
- Father Christmas
- an Easter rabbit

5 When do French people kiss under the mistletoe?
- Valentine's Day
- Christmas
- New Year's Eve

6 When might you find a paper fish pinned on your back?
- 1 April
- 1 November
- 31 December

7 Which is found in a galette des rois?

- a charm
- a paper hat
- fruit

8 Which is the French holiday-maker's favourite destination?

- the city
- the countryside
- the seaside

Look back through the book to check your answers.

INTERESTING WEBSITES

- **Listen to a French song about a birthday:** http://www.songsforteaching.com/french/z/lanniversaire.php

- **Try some French Christmas recipes:** http://noel.momes.net/recette-noel/

- **Watch a video clip about a festival in a French village in the south of France:** http://www.bbc.co.uk/learningzone/clips/marseille-la-st-eloi/5706.html

- **Find out more about Easter traditions in France:** http://www.euroclubschools.org/page36.htm

- **See a map of France and find out about different holiday regions:** http://www.frenchentree.com/regions-france-holiday/

- **Play a game to improve your geography of France:** http://primarygamesarena.com/redirect.php?id=2106

- **Make a carnival mask:** http://www.momes.net/coloriages/carnaval/carnaval.html

TRANSLATIONS

Pages 8–9

Mon jour préféré My favourite day

Bon anniversaire, Romain!
Happy birthday, Romain!

Qu'est-ce que tu as eu pour ton anniversaire?
What did you get for your birthday?

Pour mon anniversaire, j'ai eu des cartes, des cadeaux et de l'argent.
For my birthday I got cards, presents and money.

C'est génial! It's great!

J'ai eu un gâteau, avec des bougies.
I had a cake with candles.

Pour mon anniversaire, j'ai eu un jeu vidéo.
For my birthday, I got a video game.

Et toi ? Qu'est-ce que tu as eu pour ton anniversaire? Complète.
What about you? What did you have for your birthday? Complete the sentence.

Pour mon anniversaire, j'ai eu…
For my birthday, I had…

Pages 12–13

C'est Noël! It's Christmas!

Qu'est-ce que tu fais à Noël? Léo?
What do you do at Christmas, Léo?

On décore un grand sapin de Noël.
We decorate a big Christmas tree.

C'est beau! It's beautiful!

Et on a des cadeaux de Noël!
And we have Christmas presents!

On décore la maison.
We decorate the house.

J'ai des cadeaux de Noël.
I get Christmas presents.

J'adore les cadeaux!
I love presents.

Et toi? Qu'est-ce qu tu fais à Noël?
What about you? What do you do at Christmas?

À Noël, chez moi, on…
At Christmas, in my house, we…

Pages 16–17

Les fêtes d'hiver Winter celebrations

Antoine, chez toi, il y a des fêtes en hiver? Antoine, where you live, are there celebrations during the winter?

Oui. En hiver, il y a la Fête des Rois.
Yes. In winter, there's the Festival of the Three Kings.

Cette année, j'ai eu la fève.
This year, I got the charm.

La galette des rois, c'est bon!
'Kings' cake' is good!

La couronne The crown

Chez toi, il y a des fêtes en hiver?
Where you live are there celebrations during the winter?

Chez moi, il y a... Where I live, there is...

Pages 20–21

La fête nationale The national holiday

Salut, Carine! Ton pays a une fête nationale?
Hallo, Carine! Does your country have a national holiday?

Oui! En France, la Fête Nationale, c'est le quatorze juillet.
Yes! In France, the national holiday is on 14 July.

Il y a des défilés, des bals, des feux d'artifice... et des pétards!
There are parades, dances, firework displays... and firecrackers!

Le drapeau tricolore est un symbole de la Révolution française.
The French flag is a symbol of the French Revolution.

Le quatorze juillet, il y a des feux d'artifice en France.
On 14 July, there are firework displays in France.

Ton pays a une fête nationale?
Does your country have a national holiday?

Oui, c'est le... Yes, it's the...

Non. No.

Pages 24–25

Les vacances d'été The summer holidays

Romain, quelle est ton activité préférée pendant les grandes vacances?
Romain, what's your favourite activity during the summer holidays?

Pendant les grandes vacances, j'aime me reposer.
During the summer holidays, I like to relax.

En juillet, je vais en colonie de vacances.
In July, I go to summer camp.

C'est génial! It's great!

J'aime faire du bricolage avec mon père.
I like to do DIY with my dad.

Je fais du canoë avec mes amis.
I go canoeing with my friends.

Et toi? Quelle est ton activité préférée pendant les grandes vacances?
What about you? What's your favourite activity during the summer holidays?

J'aime... I like...

INDEX

TEST YOUR FRENCH

Can you remember what these words mean?

1 des cadeaux: cards? presents? candles?

2 un sapin de Noël: a Christmas decoration? a Christmas tree? a Christmas cake?

3 des crêpes: pancakes? eggs? cakes?

1 presents 2 a Christmas tree 3 pancakes